The Spiritual Awakening of a Spray Tanner

By

CARLA SAVANNAH

Copyright © 2017 by Carla Savannah Book Cover design by Kristie Bradfield

www.kristiebradfield.com

This book is protected by copyright. No part of it may be reproduced, stored in a retrieval system, or transmitted in any form or by any means, electronic, mechanical, photocopying, recording, or otherwise, without the prior written permission of the author.

ISBN: **978-0-648-00104-1**

Contents

Introduction — 7

Chapter 1 — 13
The Spray Tanning Journey Begins

Chapter 2 — 25
Becoming the best spray tanner

Chapter 3 — 30
Lesson 1 – Establishing Boundaries

Chapter 4 — 41
Lesson 2 – Not all help is welcomed

Chapter 5	50

Lesson 3 – Life is so precious!

Chapter 6	58

Lesson 4 – Presence and Peacefulness

Chapter 7	65

Lesson 5 – Uniqueness and Beauty of each Woman

Chapter 8	70

My Spiritual Growth

Chapter 9	82

Lesson 6 – Like attracts Like

Chapter 10	88

The Ugliness of the Beauty Industry

Chapter 11   98

Counselling under the most uncomfortable circumstances

Conclusion   105

Introduction

I chose to write this book as an example of how the most unlikely or unexpected career changes can ultimately still lead you to your life's purpose. If your life purpose is to help people, the Universe will create a way to put you on the right path so that you can help people.

I've always felt like mothering and/or nurturing was my purpose for being on this Earth. For years I accepted that my way of fulfilling this mission was to simply be a Mother. Foolishly thinking that simply being a Mother was the easy way to do it. I studied Psychology and did my Diploma in Counselling with a Major in Marriage, Relationship and Conflict resolution Counselling. This opened up a door for me that ignited my passion for the human psyche, to helping people in other ways besides parenting them. But when I became a spray tanner I never imagined that this would be "the" career that would test my counselling skills the most and encourage the most growth within me.

The challenges I faced and lessons I learnt through my experiences as a spray tanner gave me valuable insight into Women and most importantly myself.

Once a lady who came into the Salon where I was tanning at the time and knowing me as not one to pass up an opportunity, while she was sitting down getting her hair done I took the chance to show her my first book I had recently published called "How do I know when I'm ready to have kids …and more kids?" The lady flicked briefly through my book and said "and what makes you qualified to write about this subject?" in a very insistent and blunt sort of way. Every part of my being felt like saying to her "My experience!" however, when I took a moment to process her energy and body language I almost said "What kind of answer are you looking for?" But I knew what she was looking for. She was wanting me to give her a formal qualification so that's what I politely gave her, I answered "I have my Diploma in Professional Counselling with a major in Marriage/Relationship and conflict resolution."

I felt slightly insecure and a little sad that my experiences and suffering with Post Natal Depression wasn't a good enough reason or "qualification" to give me rights to write a book about the importance of conscious pre-parenting and thinking carefully before deciding to have kids. Society expects that if you don't have a high status or qualification in what you are writing about then what you are writing about is not to be valued as creditable advice. I'd like to think that people would like to get parenting advice from someone who knows what the challenges of parenting are because they've experienced and overcome those challenges themselves.

Furthermore, it's amazing how within my Spray Tanning career some ladies treated me as though I was a low class servant because I was just a "Spray Tanner". Only when they found out that I had a "Counselling" qualification did they bother to treat me with a little more respect and give me the time of day. This was strange to me after all I wasn't any different, I was still the same person that was putting cream on their hands and feet and spraying them the week before.

I felt sure that one day I was going to write a book about my journey as a Spray Tanner as this was another of my biggest growth promoting journeys outside of my studies and personal parenting challenges. I hope you will find inspiration and some enlightenment within my story.

I'll also provide some thought provoking questions throughout this book with some space for you to write your own thoughts and answers so as to encourage some of your own personal changes and evolution.

Chapter 1

The Spray Tanning Journey Begins

A high school friend of mine was talking to me about doing spray tanning from home on weekends for some extra income. I was a little confused as to why She was considering this as she was a Psychologist with a very high profile job within the government. I just assumed she was looking for some type of change or variation to her life and I didn't really bother to ask too many questions why. I'm not the type to stick my nose in other people's business unless they seem interested in sharing personal details with me. Anyways, I thought this was a great idea for someone like me who had 2 young children at the time and was looking to do something from home that was less emotionally draining than the Counselling and Parenting support which was what I was doing. So I said to her "OK since you live north of the river and I live south I'll take on the South of the river clients and I'll send all the North of the River clients to you." I figured that was there wouldn't be an overlap and none of us would feel like we are taking clients from each other.

I bought myself a machine and a tent online excited to consider how easy it was to get equipment and ordered some product on ebay. I experimented on family members and am slightly embarrassed to say I made my sweet accommodating Mother-in-law look extremely orange. I was slightly disappointed to find out that there was much more of an art to spray tanning than what I had originally thought. There's different chemicals, products, skin types, techniques, equipment and more.

My friend whom I mentioned earlier was smarter she booked in some training with a great company that was just establishing its name within the spray tanning industry and I was happy to be one of her models. That way I also got an idea of how it's done and taught.

She sprayed me in her garage and I was impressed to see just how quick it was to apply. I immediately started to do the calculations in my head of how many girls I could fit in in one day and how much money I could make. After feeling very motivated I booked in for some training sessions of my own. This was the best idea as it was very helpful and informative. The Trainer gave me the confidence I needed to actually begin getting my name out there as a Spray Tan Technician.

I advertised everywhere I could post details about my business. I went onto every free directory and created listings everywhere, posted like crazy on Facebook and created a Google presence.

I enjoyed tanning and experimenting with tanning so much that I lived and breathed it literally. I spoke about tanning to everyone I met and offered free tans and discounts everywhere. I just wanted to tan as many people as possible just to learn

about how to create that perfect tan. I set up my tent in my backyard while still trying to make sure privacy was acknowledged for my clients.
Little did I know there was so much more to running a spray tanning business than just spraying someone with a product.

It's amazing how much attention a cheap spray tan can attract. I was confused as to why girls would opt to go for a cheaper tanner rather than a quality professional tanner especially when it's for a special occasion. But there is a lot of competition in the industry especially since sunbeds and solariums have now been made illegal in Australia. This worked well in my favor in the beginning as I needed the experience and was very honest about the fact that I was still learning and starting up my business. So as to not disappoint the girls if I didn't do the most professional job in the world. Within a couple of months I had already spray tanned quite a few girls and I was well on my way to building a name for myself.

My first big eye opening experience within the tanning industry was an interesting one. I had a client who came to me for a tan but was unhappy with the conditions and environment in which I was tanning in. As I said it was in my back yard as the fumes and chemicals get everywhere and I wanted to keep my children safe. Plus, I didn't have a garage to do it in. My only other option would have been the bathroom but again wasn't a great option as it was very small with little ventilation and the product would make the tiles slippery and dangerous. This client contacted a company whose products I was using to complain that she didn't feel she had enough privacy.

The company owner contacted me to inform me of this complaint. I was very quick to take action and my Husband was wonderful enough to build a private room for me on our front patio. I used my Lounge room as a waiting room for clients and it was all enclosed private area for me to spray tan. Once a week I could roll up the plastic shutters and open up the whole area to use a high pressure hose to clean out the whole room ready for a new week of tanning.

It wasn't long before the second complaint came in but I was slightly more prepared for this one. I was still learning how to clean out my spray guns properly but obviously I was still not doing it well as the second complaint was from a client who got a very uneven tan from my gun which the mist kept turning itself on and off. I remember trying my best to fix it and be thorough very aware at that point that the tan might not turn out too great and even. I did offer her at the time to return for a free tan in case it didn't turn out well. She was so unhappy that she went to the main company of the same product I got the first complaint from.

I tell you the second complaint didn't go down well with the owner. The owner called me up very upset questioning my tanning abilities saying she was unsure about what to do in this situation and expressed that she was tempted to not sell me her product anymore. She let me off with a warning and said that if she receives another complaint that she will no longer sell me her product.

Well, as you can imagine this didn't sit too well with me and I felt very unfairly treated as I did everything I could to make sure my clients where happy. I understood her position, she was building a great company and didn't want anyone to put a bad name on her products. But all I thought was If this Woman takes the product away from me then how can I run my tanning business? She can potentially put me out of work when technically I'm running my own business this shouldn't be a risk. I began to do a lot of research. I was excited to find that the world of tanning was much bigger than I ever imagined. There was a world of different suppliers and products out there and every time I contacted a new company they were delighted to help and sell me as much of their product as possible. This is where all the doors opened for me.

I bought samples from everywhere I could get my hands on a product. I experimented, mixed, researched and played with every type of product, technique and skin type I could. I was determined to become the best spray tanner ever! My Ego was bruised and I wouldn't have someone firing me from my very own business.

I finally perfected my technique. I found a handful of products I really liked, I tanned every 15 mins and was happy to provide the variety of various products on my shelf. That became what I was well known for. Variety of products for all different skin types, my logo displayed "Because your skin is Unique!" This worked out well as I didn't have to be exclusive to only one company and I had various companies doing all the advertising for me. I was listed on the stockist list of various big companies so they technically did most of the hard advertising work for me. The clients began rolling in, But, like I said before there's so much more to spray tanning and running your own business than people know.

Thought provoking Question 1:

What inspires you to get out of bed in the morning? What do you love to do? What did you love to do as a child?

Chapter 2

Becoming the best spray tanner

After perfecting my technique, finding all the right products to work with and mastering the art of spray tanning my business seemed to be growing rapidly. Upon talking to other spray tanners and comparing my influx of clients to other spray tanners I began to realize my business was growing at a much faster rate than every other tanner. The average spray tanning business would average 7 regular clients per week by the end of their first year. This number is supposed to go up by 7 each year. By the end of my first year I was already averaging 15 clients per week by the second year I was averaging 25-30 per week. Within 3 years of having opened my business I got very fast and I was spray tanning every 10 mins. The most I could fit into one day was 55-60 girls/tans. The only reason why I didn't do more is because my body, my wrist and my lungs weren't coping.

I began to ask myself what makes me different from other spray tanners? Why is it that I'm growing so rapidly as opposed to other tanners. I questioned my clients asking them what they liked most about my spray tans?. Amongst some of the answers I was given was "Because you care!" "Because you take pride in your work!" "Because you have a mothering and comforting energy about you" As a matter of fact I began to look back at how many times Ladies would come into my tan room upset or crying and they would always leave feeling more settled, happy and with a sense of hope. That was a pivotal moment where a light bulb went off in my head, I was still doing my Counselling work even within my spray tanning service. Lots of ladies were seeking me out because I was technically offering more than just a spray tan. I was offering encouragement and empowerment to these beautiful Women.

When girls come into a tan room they are put in one of the most vulnerable positions they could be in. They are removing all their clothes to reveal to the tanner everything they would call their imperfections. These imperfections that I would see as Uniqueness. I could see these beautiful Women in a way that they wouldn't allow many people to see them. They trusted me and I was humbled to be put in that position of trust with their vulnerability.

I became a great spray tanner because I did care! Not just about how the spray tan looked and creating the perfect tan for their special occasion but I cared about how my clients felt when they walked in, when they were put in the situation of having to take their clothes off and when they left. This was a moment of awakening for me. I knew I had an opportunity to make a difference in the lives of Women within a simple 10 min Spray Tan slash Counselling session.

Thought provoking Question 2

What are your favorite qualities about yourself?

Chapter 3

Lesson 1 – Establishing Boundaries

I became pregnant with my 3rd child after about 2 or 3 years of tanning. I had quite a few health complications within this pregnancy (none of them to do with my spray tanning career) and faced the dilemma of whether I should continue to Spray tan. This would mean I'd have to breathe in all the chemicals while I was pregnant and my body was going to become that little more exhausted. Unfortunately, I needed an income so I had very little choice over the matter. I had to continue tanning but just took extra precautions such as wearing thicker masks and buying an extra 3 extraction units to keep the room clear of chemicals while I worked.

I spray tanned myself to exhaustion. I accepted client after client not taking into consideration my physical sluggishness. I would say to my clients that if I went into labor while I was tanning they would have to be prepared to take me straight to the hospital. As this was my 3rd I didn't know how fast the labor was going to go. I had heard that labors are quicker and quicker each time.

Around Christmas time I was extremely busy but made sure I had Christmas Day and Boxing Day with my family. I had clients messaging me last minute on Christmas morning requesting a tan. When I received these messages on Christmas day I was at a bit of a loss for words and never knew how to reply without sounding shocked at the request. I'd write "I'm sorry but I'm unable to tan you today, Merry Christmas" but what I really felt like saying was "Sure, how about you come and open the Christmas presents with my children and eat Christmas breakfast with us too!" or "Well if you were married with children would you mind if I came to your house on Christmas morning to ask for you to stop everything with your family so I could make use of your services?" Obviously I saw these occasions differently to some other people.

I had an interesting experience that summer. There was a client who called me at 6am in the morning saying her current tanner had cancelled on her last minute and begged that I tan her that morning. Even though I was very booked out and tired from the pregnancy and looking after my older kids I decided to squeeze her in at 8am before getting my kids up and off to school, which was something I would often do. I figured I could squeeze everything in all the time, work and family.

I had finished spray tanning a couple of clients and the client who'd called me that early in the morning still hadn't showed. I spray tanned in my front patio which was enclosed but was outdoors and right near my front door. So I'd never miss a client I could see anyone who pulled into my driveway through the curtains as a silhouette and anyone could hear me tanning and talking to my clients. So I was sure she still hadn't come. I was 8 months pregnant and slow to answer the door but still not that slow to have missed a client.

Next thing I knew I get at abusive SMS saying that I had wasted her time. She called me every abusive name under the Sun. I said to her "I'm sorry but you must have gone to the wrong house or something as I didn't hear or see anyone coming to my front door" She proceeded to call me a "rude bitch" amongst a few other things, I tried calling her to tell her there must be some misunderstanding and that I was there still waiting to tan her but she ignored my calls and told me to not bother calling her again and that she would never return again. I made every effort to fit her tan in even though I was very exhausted with 2 kids at home getting ready for school, 8 months pregnant and tanning which obviously was no bother to her.

I found that each year brought me common messages or similar lessons. I'd get Women booking in and not showing up or coming so late that any commitments I'd have after their tans would be ruined, I'd have girls coming to get tans then not having the money to pay for their tans or only half the money or I'd have girls who would purposely sabotage the after care of their tan simply so they could get free tan next time.

It was that year that made me realize that some people don't take home businesses seriously and don't respect the privacy of a home business. Even after telling people I couldn't spray tan on a specific day because it was either Christmas, my child's birthday or my wedding anniversary they wouldn't respect my "No" answer and still insist and push to get a spray tan when they wanted it. There were even some people who I'd notify that I couldn't tan them at a specific time and they would still purposely come to my home or arrive at my home 30mins earlier than their appointment to their own convenience. So either I was forced to tan them before I was ready to or I'd have to leave them sitting in my Lounge room watching TV while I fed my children or cooked dinner.

My husband always felt uncomfortable sitting in the Lounge room with clients especially considering most of my clients where in robes, pajamas or not wearing any underwear, so as soon as a client arrived he'd designate himself to the back of the house with my kids so I could focus on my clients and my work. I'd feel terrible as he worked everyday day and wasn't even able to rest on his own couch in the evenings because I was working from home and the house was always full of Women.

I was mostly flexible and always tried to make an effort to fit Ladies in where I could sometimes even when I couldn't, But, That was the year where I learnt about personal boundaries and learnt to establish some ground rules within my home business. Not only was my personal boundaries too flexible but it was obviously bleeding out into my business also. People weren't respecting me, my family or my home. If I wanted to become a serious business owner this was a challenge I needed to overcome both in my personal life and within my business.

I began to go over all my steps and notice where I had been too flexible or unclear about my expectations from those I interacted with. After all if you're not 100% clear with people about what you will or won't tolerate people can always turn around to you and say they didn't know right! I learnt to be confident with what I said and demand to be treated with respect. My "No" became a strong high quality No! Without Ego and full of compassion for myself and others. My messages became very clear and to the point. I spoke with clear intention. I wasn't rude I always kept polite and to the point but people knew in my tone that I wasn't going to tolerate rudeness, lack of integrity or rule bending on my time.

It was around this time that I established a payment method to have girls make payment before their appointment. That way I didn't have to worry about losing appointments, I could buy products needed for the spray tans and also it helped to weed out the people who were serious about showing up for their spray tans and those who were just penciling in an appointment not really intending to keep their appointment. The business began to run more smoothly and income was more secure and predictable.

Challenge and Lesson Number 1 tackled successfully. Personal boundaries and Respect established!

Thought provoking Question 3

Can you think of a time when you said yes to someone when you really wanted to say No? Would you do it differently today? Why and How?

Chapter 4

Lesson 2 – Not all help is welcomed

Within the Spray tanning profession, the tanner gets to see a lot of what most people don't see. We see the cuts, the scars, the bruises and everything most people are able to hide from the rest of the world. We see the tears resolve into smiles and the smiles dissolve into tears.

I had one amazing client and good friend called Bec, who overcame some incredibly hard relationship challenges. Bec was mistreated not only emotionally but physically. She didn't have much confidence within herself or her body. I saw her shed many tears and many stories before she finally gained the courage to leave an abusive relationship she was in. Her new found freedom left her a little lost for a while but she soon began to take care of herself again.

Bec started to work out at the Gym and I watched her progress in self-esteem and body confidence. I joked around with her that one day she would be competing in fitness competitions on stage. Her answer to me was "No way, I could never do that!" Within a couple of months guess what? She was prepping for Fitness competitions. She went on to win trophy after trophy, did calendar shoots, was in fitness magazines and so much more! The transformation within this woman within a short period of a few months was extraordinary! I put it down to her amazing strength and willpower! Sometimes I speak to her today about her transformation. It still gives me that warm fuzzy feeling of hope for humanity. If only every Woman had half the determination this Woman had we'd have a world full of happier more confident Women.

On another hand that year I had another regular client whom had a tendency towards what seemed to be a deep form of depression and had spoken to me of her issues with regards to a Man using her for green card then hitting the road once he'd got permanent residency within Australia. She felt fooled and you could tell her spirit was very broken with regards to relationships. Her confidence looked very bruised and she often mentioned her unwillingness to live at times. One day she didn't show up for her spray tan which was unlike her. I sent her messages to which she didn't reply to. I got very concerned as she didn't contact me for days to let me know that she was ok. I prayed that nothing had happened to her. She was inactive on Facebook so I even tried contacting people she knew to see if they'd heard from her. She contacted me soon after that to let me know she was OK. Straight after that she blocked and removed me from her friends list and hasn't made contact with me ever again since.

I was a bit thrown back by this as I was genuinely concerned for her welfare. When a regular client you've been tanning for a while that always shows up is a no show and doesn't contact you for a few days you begin to worry. Looking back I don't know whether I was right to contact her friends to see if she was ok (even though I didn't give out any personal information, I just simply stated that she didn't show for a tan which she normally is good with showing up and that she wasn't replying to my messages) or if I should have just left it. I'm still not sure if it was the right thing to do. Either way lesson 2 was in the process of manifesting itself.

A scary experience within my tanning career also happened that year. I was spray tanning a client whom as I was tanning the colour seemed to drain from her face and lips. I looked and her very attentively and asked "Are you OK?" within seconds she said "I don't think so" and she fainted. I had enough time to drop my spray gun and catch her under the arms. I sat her down on the floor and got her a glass of water. After delving deeper into her story she mentioned that she was trying to breastfeed her baby but was struggling with her breastfeeding and parenting experience. She mentioned that she was having some problems with her unsupportive partner and was feeling very emotionally and physically drained. Mostly due to a demanding lifestyle and baby. She hadn't eaten or drank anything all day. I put the fainting down to this basic information she was dehydrated. I didn't allow her to leave till she'd had a little more colour on her face. By this time I'd already completed my Breastfeeding Counselling and Birthing Doula course so I was able to give her some advice.

I checked up on her a week later to see if she was ok and if she wanted some parent support to help her get her breastfeeding back on track as this was my background before spray tanning. She just shrugged me off and said "My partner and I have decided that we don't want to breastfeed anymore" In my heart it felt like it was her partner's influence over her decision because while in my tan room she seemed keen to keep up with the breastfeeding but expressed some concern that her partner wouldn't approve.

At this point lesson number 2 became very apparent. Don't offer help or try to help anyone who doesn't want your help!! I realized that each girl has her own journey to go through. All I can do is offer support and be there if they need. At the end of the day there will be people willing to make big changes in their life just like Bec and people who are completely unwilling to change! You can lead a horse to water but you can't make it drink! I now choose very carefully where I direct my help and attentiveness. When you are a caring person the hardest thing to do is turn your back on someone and admit that maybe you can't help them, but sometimes trying to help robs them of their opportunity to grow from their own personal mistakes, lessons and experiences. Sadly, not all help is welcomed help.

Thought provoking Question 4

Do you believe in stepping back and allowing people to make their own mistakes and learn from their own consequences? Or do you feel the constant urge to have your input and opinion?

Chapter 5

Lesson 3 – Life is so precious!

Lesson 3 is the most sorrowful lesson I've learnt. I had an amazing beautiful client called Leanne who had been fighting cancer for years. Every time she overcame it the Cancer would come back stronger than the last time. Her daughter Olivia was also a client of mine. She was a teenager at the time I started tanning her and her mum. Leanne spoke to me of how she worried about her daughter being so young and what would happen to Olivia when her Mum, Leanne passes away. Olivia wasn't very close to her dad so Leanne asked that I keep an eye out for her daughter. I think that deep down she knew she may not last much longer and was doing what she could to make sure her daughter would be looked out for. She was making lots of final decisions in her life at the time tying up all loose ends before her passing.

When Leanne would get aggressive Chemo her skin would begin to get extremely dry and flake off. When she would take her clothes off in my tan room the air would be filled with the dust of her skin flying around the room when she shook her shirt. I noticed the deterioration dramatically as I didn't see her too often each time there was a noticeable difference in her. I prayed for a miracle as she was such a beautiful person and Olivia really needed her mother. Unfortunately, this was a fight she couldn't win. She really was an amazing mother and an angel.

After Leanne's passing I adopted Olivia as a little sister and she was like an auntie to my kids. I continue to advise her like a mother knowing that I could never replace that incredible Woman she called Mum!

Another client whom also reminded me of the preciousness of life was a Lady who has a rare form of Leukemia. Which took away her hearing. She was a slightly luckier Lady as the Leukemia was controllable with medication and did not need such aggressive treatment such as Chemo. She had the blessing of having a beautiful healthy baby girl. I was overjoyed as this was a happier ending to my previous experiences with Cancer and Leukemia.

Yet another beautiful "young" client of mine who used to love going to the Solarium was at a routine checkup at her doctor when the doctor noticed a spot. The Doctor mentioned that it didn't look good and insisted that she go and get it checked. It turned out to be a Melanoma that resulted in her not only removing part of her glands but after further testing they had noticed it had spread to other parts of the body and had to remove more glands. This has caused a great deal of anxiety and stress with the array of unexpected testing and surgeries needed in such a short period of time. She was very lucky to have such an alert doctor.

I've got clients who've survived serious Car accidents where the cars were unrecognizable, one Lady who survived a hit and run accident that was left for dead on the side of the road and many freak one off accidents for example a lady who had drank too much at her sister's wedding fell over and broke her neck on a side walk. She was unable to walk for months and feared she would never walk again, some have lost limbs and some are lucky to be walking but the scars on their body still remain to tell the stories. I've had Women come in with bruises all over their body and I can always tell whether it's because they drank too much and had a big night out or whether it was domestic violence. Hand and finger marks around arms, wrists and neck are virtually impossible not to distinguish from every day bumps.

I've learned to tell what type of surgery someone has had based on the scars they have. I know when someone has had breast reductions, when they've had gall bladder's removed, when they've had implants you name it after spray tanning over 3000 girls I think I've literally seen everything.

Some of the horrific stories I've heard of and seen the proof of are enough to make me grateful for what I have and happy that my arms, legs and spine are still have intact.

Then there are the numerous clients that have attempted suicide and have lived to tell their story of abuse, hurt, sadness or self-hate. These scars are the hardest to hide and the hardest for my heart to take. My heart cries for so many of these Women.

Lesson number 3. Life is so precious! It can all be gone in a heartbeat! Treat every moment as if it were your last! Appreciate what you have right now. Tomorrow is uncertain the only thing that is certain is what you have right now.

Thought provoking Question 5

If you knew this was going to be the last day you were going to be alive what would you want to do?

Chapter 6

Lesson 4 – Presence and Peacefulness

Lesson number 4 came from within me. I started to notice that no matter what happened throughout my day, whether I had a disagreement with my husband, whether my children had had a particularly active day and I was exhausted from looking after them or whether I was feeling unwell I always, ALWAYS did everything possible not to cancel any spray tans. So I began to realize just how much I loved my work. Being at work gave me a time out away from the kids, I was having adult conversations with other Ladies and I felt as though I was helping Women look and feel good. I was getting an instant feeling of appreciation and gratitude from my clients which only made me want to work more. Through spray tanning I was feeling closer to fulfilling my purpose! The care for and nurture people into evolving and growing.

When I was at work I didn't think of anything else. I felt a sense of being completely present and I was at peace. This was something I rarely ever felt within my life. I would only occasionally get a glimpse of this feeling of presence and peace when

I was watching my children sleep or joyfully playing. When I was tanning my whole focus was on what I was doing. Girls would come in with new piercings or tattoos, But, because I was so absorbed in what I was doing and on giving the perfect tan I rarely noticed new bodily accessories.

I began to think of Eckhart Tolle's book "A new Earth" where he teaches about presence and being in the Now! While I was at work it was one of the rare times in my life that I was completely in the Now! I would forget any argument or challenge I had throughout the day. If I was feeling unwell I would actually gain strength at the thought of being able to tan and talk to my clients. If I had a very stressful anxious day my work would calm me down. I was completely present and there with my client, eager to please and be of service. I felt as though no Ego existed within me when I was spray tanning. I was there to make the client happy and that's all I wanted to do at that moment in time. I would forget that I was even in my body, it's like I was expressing or projecting myself by spraying on the perfect tan. It was my master piece and how I could also express my artistic qualities creatively. A couple of times I had spray tanned some panel beater boys and they commented that I was better with a spray gun than most panel beaters. The more in Love I grew with my work the more clients I attracted.

Lesson number 4 was presence, awareness and being so much in the Now that past or future didn't exist at that moment.

I proceeded to learning slowly how to apply this lesson to other parts of my life. With my children was the next natural step. I would watch my baby with endless attention and presence. It's as though the world around me seemed to drop away and all that was there was me and my baby. I made the most of these moments.

I also began to slow down while driving. I was always such a rev head always in a hurry to get from A to B. The constant anxiety of needing to be somewhere and do something began to go away the more I became present, and thankfully so did all the speeding fines.

There were moments where I understood exactly what peace was and what peace felt like. It was that feeling of not needing to be anywhere else but right where I was and as though everything was exactly where it needs to be and as it is. It's like a feeling of surrender, acceptance and allowing all at the same time. It feels so effortless.

Thought provoking Question 6

Stop what you are doing for a few minutes to simply observe yourself in the World. Can you feel your pulse, smell your skin, look at the lines on the back of your hands, taste what's in your mouth, hear the sounds around you? How aware are you of what's happening to you and around you without judgement?

Chapter 7

Lesson 5 – Uniqueness and Beauty of each Woman

I had one lady come in once that just blew my mind. She was a larger lady but boy was her Charisma larger. Her energy was so beautiful it's hard to put into words how she lit up the room with her smile. She said to me "I'm big and fat and

I'm beautiful and I don't care what you think you still have to see and spray tan my big hairy Poonani!" She laughed and made me laugh along with her!

Her confidence and acceptance of herself radiated from her pores! Out of the thousands of clients I've tanned in my lifetime she was one that stuck in my mind and it makes me smile every time I think of her.

The more I spray tanned the more every "body" just looked like a body to me and the more indifferent I became to the image of the human body. Interestingly this rubbed off on me because I began to notice that I could go for weeks without have looked at a mirror. Sometimes I would leave the house within even looking in the mirror to do my hair.

I can't consider myself a scruffy person who doesn't care about her appearance but I did start to care less about what people thought about me and my appearance. My daughter used to call me fat, or hippopotamus, Gloria from Madagascar but honestly it never phased me. I just didn't see myself that way.

My self-confidence grew as I learned to love and respect every shape and size of a Woman. There were times when I watched my diet and began to lose some weight because I was having some health complications. When I had my gallbladder removed and some of my health issues began to settle I went back to my normal diet again. Today I'm aware of my diet for the purpose of either getting healthier or to help enhance my intuitive abilities. Seldom do I look in the mirror and see myself as overweight and feel the urge to diet to lose weight. I'm the opposite to someone suffering of Anorexia.

Lesson number 5, Love your unique body. You only get one! If you constantly compare yourself to everyone else you may never be happy within your own skin. I imagine that not being happy within yourself or in your own company must be one of the most painful things to have to live with on a daily basis. After all, if you don't love yourself why should anyone else

Thought provoking Question 7

Throughout the day ask yourself before you do anything or make any decision "What would someone that loves and respects themselves do in this situation?"

Chapter 8

My Spiritual growth

The business was starting to get so busy and having clients over with 3 kids and my husband at home, the home got very crowded and noisy while I was trying to work. I finally accepted that it was time to move the business out of home.

A client of my mine called Michele, who ran her Feng Shui Workshops from her Wellness and Healing Centre down the road from my home, just so happened to send me an SMS looking to get a spray tan for her daughter. It was at the exact time in my life that I was contemplating moving my business out of home. I asked her if she would be willing to allow me to rent a room off her at the Wellness Centre for a reasonable weekly rent. Even though I only had to work 2-3 days a week I wanted to rent weekly so that I didn't have to move my equipment back and forth each week.

Michele was amazing and very flexible. She was keen to have me around and I was happy to have a great business lady backing me up and supporting me.

When I went to check out the room I noticed that they had Counsellors, Reiki masters, a Medium and various other natural therapies there along with lots of space for workshops. As my background was within Counselling and I intended to eventually get back into doing Women's Empowerment Workshops this place was the ideal place for me to run all my businesses from. I also did Tarot Readings and Reiki Healings occasionally. Again this was the ideal place for my spiritual healings too and I felt like I was in my element around like minded people. So accepted her offer and moved my tanning to the furthest back room of the Centre.

The Medium, Anthony Grezelka would do regular séances there. One night while I was tanning Anthony was doing a Séance in the main seminar room and all the lights started flashing. Suddenly we heard a loud noise and all the lights went out! My clients and I freaked out! We joked that Anthony's power blew some lights out that night which actually turned out to be the truth went I went back in the next day. I definitely didn't stick around that night to find out what had happened! Lol! As soon as I finished all my clients I left there quick smart.

I did some Psychic Development workshops with Anthony and found him to be an amazing down to earth teacher. Anthony looked and reminded me so much of my dad whom I'd lost a few years earlier, he even has the same name so working around Anthony was sort of comforting for me. Anthony was very tolerant of all my loud tanning equipment and noisy clients. He never once complained when he probably had good reason to sometimes. Unfortunately, not everyone in the area was that kind and tolerant. There was always disagreements over parking spots and every time my clients made a little noise a couple of the therapists would get upset at my clients. My clients could no longer bring in their kids in case they make too much noise for the other practitioners.

Long story short my clientele slowly started to feel unwelcome and the business that I had poured my heart into, to create the perfect homely welcoming environment was no longer. Without clientele the weekly rent was hard to make. I rented there for 1 year. Unfortunately, the place wasn't ideal for spray tanning, So, very disheartened I needed to consider moving on

Again as fate would have it I received a phone call from the amazing creative Lady who's always done my nails advising me that she has opened up her own Salon. She felt that the Salon wouldn't be complete without a professional such as myself working along side her and made me an offer I couldn't refuse.

I felt torn at the fact that I was leaving a place that was ideal for the direction I wanted my career to take in the future which was the work more within Women's Support, Counselling and Parenting Support. This was what I studied and was qualified for. If I was to leave I would be taking one step backwards. Going back into the Beauty Industry technically. For a while I thought maybe I could just separate them and just do the tanning from the Salon and all other services from the Health and Wellness Centre. I did that briefly till Michele sold the Centre.

Spiritual growth has always been a huge priority for me! I've read hundreds of books and done numerous courses around Tarot/Angel Card readings, Numerology, Lucid Dreaming, Reiki and Psychic Development over the last 20 years. I love these courses not because I intend to work as a Medium (I don't feel that this was ever right for me, I'm too respectful and aware of the potential of the spirit world to play around in their backyard) but I do like having the direct connection with the Divine Source energy. Just simply being able to have that guidance and protection system sharp and alert when I need it and to be able to help others with it also.

I remember within one of my Psychic Development Workshops being taught to connect to my Spirit guides and ask for physical validation of their presence around me. While I was meditating I said to my guides to show me proof of their presence by showing me an "elephant". It was the first thing that came into my head and when I thought about it afterwards I realized how absurd it was going to be for them to show me an Elephant when I had nothing in my house that represented an Elephant and I wasn't going to the Zoo any time soon. Regardless I just trusted and left it. The next day I was going into my fridge to get something to eat and as soon as I opened there it was a big picture of an Elephant on a beer case that my husband had apparently just bought. I looked up into space and gave the thumbs up.

I tried this again a week later at a time that I was feeling a little down and needed to feel some support. Again with the validation being "Elephant" and I made sure there wasn't any beer in the fridge. A part of me thought this time I've stumped the world of spirit they'll need to prove themselves now. Amazingly I was the one that ended up looking like the fool. As fate would have it that afternoon my 3 year old came from school and pulled out a drawing she'd made for me at school and said "Look mummy I drew you an Elephant!" A tear came to my eye at the confirmation that I'm not alone. All I thought was "Ok, Good one this time I'm impressed! Thank you for not forsaking me"

I always felt that Psychology lacked that spiritual aspect. I love that I can combine and incorporate my spiritual Intuitiveness with my Counselling when working for myself.

Numerology seems to work very well for me. So I began to use my numerology as an initial way to connect with my clients energy. I would ask them during their tanning session (if I had some extra time) if they would like a quick, intuitive reading and most of them were happy to get some simple quick free guidance.

At first I couldn't give too much detail but the practice helped me build and work on my intuitive abilities as I was getting regular feedback and validation about the information I was giving. I noticed my accuracy increasing dramatically the more I was doing this. And slowly I was able to perceive more and more information. I was the rare spray tanner that offered this extra service.

I also noticed that as soon as my Ego stepped in or I started to get over confident or arrogant about my readings that my guidance system would suddenly go quiet. Humbleness was the key. If you are doing this kind of work with the right intention you will get rewarding results and feel the fulfillment of knowing that you've helped another human being for a higher purpose. This is the same mantra that can be applied to any business. If you run your business with the intention to help your clients in any way you can, your client focused work will be highly rewarded. If you are doing it simply for money, recognition of your Ego, or worldly desires you've lost the battle before it's even begun! Your business won't have much to stand on.

Thought provoking Question 8

Are you aware of any synchronicities happening or that have happened in your life? Are you aware that you have the power to create more of these?

Chapter 9

Lesson 6 – Like attracts Like

As I enhanced and opened up more of my Intuitive abilities I began to notice the most interesting synchronicities start to happen.

When I did some Psychic Development courses I learnt about Vibrational energy and how like attracts like. Some people are attracted to the same place at the same time as other people who are within a similar vibrational range to themselves. Which is usually why when you get a room full of people who don't know each other pretty soon you start to see people magnetize towards each other and creating little groups of people they have something in common with. To actually experience this within my job was amazing.

I always believed in the law of attraction but here I had the proof right in my face that I couldn't ignore. There were nights that I would have many girls with the exact same star signs, born in the same months, have the same numerology, born into similar cultures, have the same personality archetypes or there was always some common theme. For example most of those girls were trying to get pregnant or getting married and so on. It was incredible. When you have 5 girls out of 25 girls coming in that all have the same star signs for example you can put it down to coincidence, but when start getting 15 out of 25 girls coming in all with the same star signs you have to consider that there might be some bigger force or energy at play here. It has to be the Law of attraction.

Having learnt this lesson, I started to become very aware of my bookings and the people who were booking in at particular nights. I always knew whether I was going to have a smooth easy night based on which group of girls had booked in. If I had a group of girls that complained often or where very fussy I knew it was going to be a tough night, but if I had a group of high vibrational girls that were easy going and always happy I knew it was going to be and fun and simple night to get through.

I adopted this lesson quickly. I became very aware of what type of people I was attracting into my personal life as well as into my business. Every time I attracted a client who was easy going, respectful and co-operative to I was extremely grateful to the Universe for sending me such a wonderful client. But every time I would have difficult clients contact me or being rude it was a warning to me that my vibes where not very good that day and I was attracting low vibrational people.

Also when I was preparing to do Women's empowerment workshops based on the energy of the ladies that were booking in I knew whether it was going to be a great growth promoting process with a group that was going to support each other or whether it was going to be a group that was going to be negative and unable to create positive changes.

This has been a useful lesson as it's a good way for me to take personal responsibility for what kind of vibes I'm putting out there and consider carefully what I'm attracting into my life.

Thought provoking Question 9

Based on how you are feeling today what kind of events or people do you think you will attract into your life today?

Chapter 10

The Ugly side of the Beauty Industry

The Beauty industry was a contrast of emotions to work within. There are some aspects that are great to experience. Making people feel good about themselves and watching them step out of the Salon feeling pampered and confident was great. I also love being of service so this provided me with the opportunity to do this. However, on the other hand there's a lot that goes on behind the scenes that really didn't resonate with my way of being.

There were quite a few things I didn't like about the beauty industry. I realize I'm generalizing within some of the things I'm about to mention but am well aware of the fact that there is both polarities of good and bad aspects to the beauty industry. Some of the things I was exposed to that I didn't like was;

1. Girls can be very envious of other girl's success! When girls see how successful you are within the industry they stalk all your social media, find out who your clients are and attempt to contact and take your clients. They will steal your ideas and make them

their own. I've had numerous clients of mine who knew of my success and tried opening up their own spray tanning businesses. I was always one that felt strongly about the support and success of other Women.

For this reason, Women would use me to get information about how to open a business, find out what products I used, they asked me to train them in my technique and other general advice.

Unfortunately, some girls were more cunning and didn't ask me for help directly and they would get their friends to book in with me just to see my techniques or find out what products I was using to send back information to their friend. A couple of times girls have deliberately come in for a tan and would sabotage the before or after care of their spray tan in order to take photos of a so called "bad tan" just to try put down my business and make their regular tanned look good. In this industry I have a very loyal following so all the gossip always came back to my ears one way or another and I began to learn who I could and couldn't trust.

So I decided to open up a Spray tanning help and tips group where I added only the best of the best, for all Spray Tan Professionals to go onto to get help and advice around tanning. I got some help running the group from a fellow talented and knowledgeable Spray Tanner Kim, whom has her own line of products in the eastern states. This was a great idea and has been a very successful tool for tan technicians all over Australia!

2. It's a Dog eat Dog world. If you put up a post on Facebook searching for a particular service immediately you get hundreds of posts with everyone trying to undercut everyone else in the sheer desperation of getting clients. It's amazing how some girls are willing to step on other people's toes in order to try and achieve success. If I put up a price of $40 someone under will put $20 then under that will come someone offering for $10 even as low as $5 sometimes. I only ever offer a price that low if I have product that has reached it's shelf life and is about to be thrown out in which case I'd lose all that

money if I don't use it up quickly. Nonetheless this wouldn't even cover the cost of the product. People who offer such silly specials willingly obviously haven't paid to register their business or have any insurance. These girls wouldn't understand the concept of business as they are drowning and destroying their own industry by offering prices that low. To top it off they're selling themselves out. Whenever girls contacted me asking for discounts and trying to compare my prices my answer to them was "There are cheap Spray tanners out there!" I provide a quality service. I'm not going to sell myself short when I know I'm worth the service I provide.

3. I had to stop accepting Male clients for a few different reasons, mainly for safety reasons. Some Men unfortunately conduct themselves in a way that isn't appropriate when they take their clothes off. Some Men have jealous girlfriends who don't appreciate their Men taking their clothes off in front of another Woman even if it is just for a spray tan. I've had ladies sending me abusive messages simply because their partner has liked my Facebook page or a picture of one of my beautiful clients who's been tanned by me. These Women don't realize I'm a happily married, almost 40 year old Women with 4 kids running 3 businesses. I don't have time for childish girly insecurities and jealousy games and I especially don't have time to get involved with other girl's Men.

So I made the rule that I refuse to tan Men unless they come in with their partner or family member and I refuse to tan any Men unless they are wearing full briefs. P.S. On the cover of this book I'm spraying one of my male fitness clients, Junyu. I chose that picture because I couldn't think of a nicer more inspirational and genuinely nice guy that I've Spray tanned to put on my book cover.

4. The support group for Spray tanners on Facebook that I opened up with the intention of Women helping Women in the industry, Unfortunately, went through a few hick-ups. When you mix a large group of Women all with the same plans and direction in mind there's always going to be

those who are willing to support and help others and those who will try to create a hierarchy and control or push around others. The moment bitchy behavior and put downs began to occur the support group was no longer a support group and some changes needed to be made. Once everyone was on the same page and people where acting with more integrity within the group it began to run smoothly again.

There's no need to put other Women or other Businesses down simply for one's own desperation for material success or egotistical desires.

Thought provoking Question 10

Do you believe that in order to stay on top and be respected that you need to put other people down? How do you help lift other Women up?

Chapter 11

Counselling under the most uncomfortable circumstances

The thing about Spray Tanning is that you have an opportunity to see your clients under the most vulnerable circumstances. When someone takes their clothes off in front of you there is really not much more they can hide. It would take a very confident person to be able to stand in front of you naked and not feel somewhat exposed emotionally. This situation provides the perfect opportunity for healing to take place.

Which within a traditional Counselling session you need to establish connection, trust and rapor first within a Spray Tanning session all of these first steps happen within a matter of minutes. Immediately the client is expected to trust the Spray Tanner not only to do the job they're getting paid to do but they're trusting that the spray tanner will not make judgements of the client's vulnerable state at that moment in time.

The moment a person takes their clothes off for the first time they are internally analyzing and criticizing themselves. The client's thoughts are grounded in subconscious fears such as "What does this person think of me? What if they think I'm ugly, hairy or fat? What if they don't like me after seeing me naked? Will they want to tan me ever again once they see how imperfect I am? Am I normal?"

Reassuring them that all their fears are merely their own perception of themselves is the first step. Letting them know that you are there simply to get the job done and not to judge them. But what about when they've had a bad day at work, had a fight with their partner, lost their job, lost a family member and so many other scenarios that Spray tanners can be faced with? This is where things for the average person who has no basic Counselling skills can get sticky.

Here's a girl standing in front of you naked sobbing her eyes out because her boyfriend just broke up with her or has got another girl pregnant. She's feeling terribly upset and insecure and to top it off she's completely naked and emotionally vulnerable too. You have just been given the perfect opportunity to provide some healing for a girl who's already open and exposed to you but you only have 10 short minutes of speed Counselling, But what can you do if you don't have the experience and training.

This is often the case within the Beauty industry. Girls seem to find it safer to express themselves to other Women while they are getting their Beauty needs met. Hair dressing, nails, waxing, spray tans etc… Women long for counsel from other Women. When you step into a Salon you're often met with a big sense of Gossip sessions always happening. Which in so many ways is true but it's only because that's their way of getting some comfort and connection.

For this reason, I feel very strongly about Women within the beauty industry needing to do a short course or some intense units on and around Counselling before they are qualified to practice Beauty therapies.

I believe that this is one of the things that makes me different from other Spray Tanners.
My skills and background within Counselling and Supporting Women as given me some amazing tools to help Women create positive changes in their lives. Even if I only have 10 mins with these girls each week!

This has been one of the most rewarding parts of being a Spray Tanner/Intuitive Women's Counsellor. Not only seeing the changes occur and the Women growing but seeing it happen in such short periods of time with such limited opportunities. It really made me wonder why some people get Counselling sessions weekly for periods of 1 hour at a time and not able to create fast long term changes. But the answer lies within the open and vulnerable state in which the Women enter the Spray Tanning process initially. This is the advantage that the Beauty industry has over traditional professional Counselling. Who knows maybe one day Naked Counselling might be something that catches on Lol.

Thought provoking Question 11

Do you become humble and grateful when someone trusts you enough to show you their vulnerable side? Or do you take advantage of their weakness and vulnerability at the time? How do you comfort those who are in a vulnerable state around you?

Conclusion

Most of the lessons in the beginning where things I had to learn about myself. The establishing of boundaries, knowing my limits and expectations, learning to love and accept myself, learning to love my body and learning to have presence, awareness and appreciation within my world. All were for the benefit of the self.

Once most of these internal closer to home lessons where achieved I was then able to extend my awareness to the external world around me. Developing the insight to appreciate other people's stories, understanding the preciousness of life and seeing how we are all interconnected. For once I actually understood how we all needed each other and how each person plays an important role within society.

I learnt about the depth and complexity of human beings as well as the superficiality of human nature. I realized that in order to become a more conscious human being, the compassion had to start from within me first. Nurturing myself inevitably then leaked out and led me to become a more compassionate and nurturing human being naturally towards others around me.

When people today ask me what I do, I say I'm a Mum, a Spray tanner, a Counsellor, a Tarot reader, a Reiki healer, an Author, a Wife and so much more! I refuse to be defined by one single career when one single career does not accommodate for my multiple interests and passions. Earlier generations will teach you that you have to stick to and perfect one career path but recent studies show that kids being born today may have up to five different career paths within their life time. Who says we can only succeed in one career path. We are learning and expanding at a faster rate than ever before! Don't be limited by what society's view says is acceptable.

Ultimately from what I thought was going to be an easy mindless career choice that I thought I could just do while looking after my children from home actually led me in the direction of my personal evolution and life purpose anyways. How do you know what your life purpose is? Simply look back to what you enjoyed doing as a child when survival and money didn't play any part in what you chose to do. As a child I always liked to express myself in artistic creative ways as this gave my mind the space to slow down for a moment, I would love to communicate and I always loved helping and being of service to people whom appreciated my services. Today I'm doing exactly that. I'm helping people, I'm being of service, I'm being creative, I'm getting to know myself in spirit, I'm communicating and helping people through my communication skills and lucky for me, I'm getting paid for it. I'm ultimately doing a combination of everything I love to do.

I've officially experienced the true meaning to the Zen saying "When the student is ready the Teacher will appear" Buddha

How have you grown from your experiences?

Thank you! Namaste!

www.carlasavannah.com.au

Other Books by Carla Savannah

"How do I know when I'm ready to have kids …and more kids?" - 2016

Recommended Reading for personal growth

How do I know when I'm ready to have kids ...and more kids? - By Carla Savannah

A New Earth - By Eckhart Tolle

Three Magic Words - By Uell S Anderson

Power Vs Force - By David R Hawkins

The Completion Process "and" Shadows before dawn - By Teal S

Biology of Belief - By Bruce Lipton

The dark side of the light chasers - Debbie Ford

The Woman Code - By Sophia A Nelson

www.ingramcontent.com/pod-product-compliance
Lightning Source LLC
Chambersburg PA
CBHW061334040426
42444CB00011B/2915